Unlock the *Secrets* to
ORGANIZING
Your *Mind* and Your *Life*

Ni'Tasha Liggins

PAGE PUBLISHING, INC.
Conneaut Lake, PA

First originally published by Page Publishing 2021

ISBN 978-1-6624-3062-6 (pbk)
ISBN 978-1-6624-3063-3 (digital)

Printed in the United States of America

To my amazing husband, Phil, who gives selflessly, and our awesome and high-spirited children (whom we lovingly refer to as our *little people*), I dedicate this book to you. This entire writing process could not have happened without your prayers, patience, and overwhelming support. Thank you for providing me the quiet moments and life experience to develop this work. I love you all to life.

Contents

PREFACE 7

INTRODUCTION 9

01
CALENDAR DEVELOPMENT
AND ORGANIZATION 11

02
PRIORITIZATION 17

03
PROCRASTINATION AND
STAGNATION 25

04
TIME MANAGEMENT 33

05
HOW YOU START AND END 37

06
ESTABLISHING ROUTINES 41

07
THE SECRET UNLOCKED 47

Preface

The idea behind organizing your mind and organizing your life is simply the act of taking back the power and control of your time. This concept and demand to hold ownership and regain balance in life are well past due. Ask yourself the following questions. How long do I want the clock to control me? Am I tired of giving my time and energy over to the clock allowing it to dictate my life?

In this book, you will receive the key to unlocking the secrets to organizing your mind and your life. Are you up for the challenge of changing from the inside out? This change will influence and cultivate a whole new outlook on life's journey. Through tips and strategies have proven to help in the area of productive living and an organized lifestyle. You are sure to walk away from this book encouraged, invigorated, and assured, you can do this and find balance on life's journey.

Introduction

The alarm clock sounds at 6:00 a.m. I reach over toward my nightstand, tumbling through and across my jewelry box, water bottle, a ton of journals and notebooks, and at last, my hand hit the alarm and shut it off. It's time, or at least, according to the clock, it's time to wake up and get up. For the longest time, my clock has dictated my every move. At 6:00 a.m. I wake up, 6:10 a.m. prayer, meditation, and reflection, 6:30 a.m. get dressed, 6:40 a.m. wake the kids, 7:00 a.m. breakfast, and 7:40 a.m. breakfast cleanup.

This process went on and on and on. My clock ran me, it was my master, and I was its puppet. The master pulls the strings, and I dance to its every beat until I said no more. I realized I had given my clock entirely too much power over me, and suddenly, I refused to allow the clock to control me and decided to take back control over the clock.

01

CHAPTER:

CALENDAR DEVELOPMENT
AND ORGANIZATION

01

There are several building blocks to taking power and control over the twenty-four-hour clock we all run on daily. One of the essential and primary blocks to this foundation needed is the development of a calendar and the commitment to fully engage the calendar.

What is meant by *commit and fully engage the calendar*? This simply means using specific practices when placing things on the calendar and committing to following through with what you seek to accomplish on the calendar within any given day. In other words, if the scheduled event, occasion, or appointment is not relevant, necessary, or even probable, don't waste mental space or calendar space trying to fit it in. We will discuss this a little later in the book, the concept of best yes practices.

The purpose of the calendar from a general perspective is to have a glance at the week or even month ahead with regards to things going on inside and outside your home. If the calendar is used correctly and consistently, this process will serve as a great benefit to you within your home and work environment.

Calendar systematic use varies depending on the user. For some people, an actual handheld planner where the user can color-code, use stickers, or doodle in the borders work best. Others enjoy the flexibility and compatibility of using a digital calendar were some of the same features are available just in digital form.

I'm a mix between old-school, meaning *I have to write everything down* to a new school digital calendar where I can share calendars with my family. For me, the use of the digital calendar allows my husband and kids to view and share calendar events as prioritized within our home. Properly prioritizing your calendar and organizing items placed on your calendar will be beneficial in lowering stress, which comes as a direct result of overcommitting and failure to follow through with commitments made. Proper use of the calendar varies by user.

However, one good rule of thumb is not to place every single thing you do on the calendar. Viewing a calendar covered in to do's can be overwhelming for anyone. When this occurs, you run the risk of self-sabotaging and failing to complete an important task.

The most productive method used in the process of writing this book has been an organizational system that accompanies the calendar. What this looks like from a practical perspective is designating an area in your home or work space and utilizing it as a central command center. This area will be a place you frequently visit or the main space used throughout your day. For instance, in a kitchen, mudroom, home office, cubicle wall, and other locations such as these.

Because I work from home, I have created my command center in two high-frequency areas for my family and myself, the kitchen and our laundry room. Currently, I am homeschooling three of my five children; therefore, I have created one central wall in the kitchen as their curriculum wall. Everything is organized and neatly placed on this wall. Dates when assignments are due, times when Zoom class calls are required, and more. This process has removed those dates and times off my already loaded calendar.

Having a command center has also provided a centralized place for viewing by my husband and kids to allow everyone to know what is expected within each day. Some of the other material posted rather than crowding my calendar is my weekly menu, chore chart, daily routine, and important dates. Remember, I use my laundry room as a central command center as well. In the laundry room, I have placed a corkboard and dry-erase board. Both boards serve a variety of purposes included but not limited to important upcoming events, daily routine schedules, laundry schedules, and more.

Again, this visual aid assists in removing those daily functionalities or later scheduled engagements from the calendar. Ultimately, this allows the effectiveness of prioritizing to work while ensuring a productive and efficient flow is created within the command center domain.

02

CHAPTER:
PRIORITIZATION

02

As a mother of five, I realized before having kids, everything I thought was a priority is now somewhat an afterthought in the big scheme of life. Establishing and understanding your priorities in the mind and then writing these priorities out for your day, month, or year is a major component to obtaining an organized mind and life.

Priorities are different for everyone. Yes, there is no cookie-cutter approach to setting priorities, there is no one-size-fits-all. When considering organizing the mind to organize your life, we have to evaluate where we start. I would argue we start with the mind. Everything we do starts with a thought. This thought is followed by an action, and a response to the action taken. What does this mean in regards to prioritization? It means we have to put thought into how we choose to spend our time.

The thought we put into this area then shapes how productive and purposeful our actions will be. Have you ever experienced a reflective moment where you were evaluating the use of your time only to discover you accomplished absolutely nothing you set out to accomplish? I can assume I'm alone in answering yes to this question. Then again, I can only imagine there are plenty of people who have experienced this or are currently facing a failed attempt at accomplishing some goal or task set forth.

To put this in context, I would like to express the term "failure" referred to in this section of the book is not based on the result of failed attempts due to issues outside of one's control. Unforeseen circumstances and major life changes have the potential to do derail even the most mentally and physically inspired and self-motivated individual. This refers specifically to failure to fulfill a goal because of plain old procrastination (we will talk more about this in a later chapter), self-doubt, or one's unwillingness to prioritize and keep the main thing the focal point.

When we allow our calendars, schedules, and mind to be overrun by a hefty to-do list, unnecessary, and unproductive engagements we lose. We lose out on time, energy, money, happiness, and so much more. Of course, I am not telling you that placing your child in every extracurricular activity is wrong, or taking on every role or task requested by an employer or friend even when it's to your own physical and mental detriment is wrong. At one point or another, I believe we have all been there. The place where we are doing entirely too much.

I can recall a time when I walked away from a job I loved and would have sworn no one could fill my role. I managed several group homes working specifically with adults ailed with bipolar disorder and schizophrenia. My clients were the absolute best, and it was a joy serving them. But guess what, when my husband and I started our family and decided I stay home. I left my dream job of serving others, and my replacement was there within the week of my departure.

No one can indeed do what you do, you bring your own unique and creative gifts to the world. However, the world does not stop because you cannot fulfill a request. Although there is nothing wrong with extending a helping hand or ensuring your children are well-rounded by providing options. I'm simply suggesting, evaluate where and how you are prioritizing your time.

Does your current schedule benefit your family and yourself? Are there currently things on your to-do list where delegation can be implemented or items deleted altogether? Here is an opportunity for complete honesty and transparency with yourself. Is what you are doing currently with scheduling or managing time working? Balanced thoughts lead to balanced schedules, which lead to a fulfilling and balanced life.

The main question people ask when sorting through scheduling and time management is: where do I start with prioritizing and taking back control of my life? A great starting place is in your mind. All of your thoughts, ideas, decisions, and presumptions start in your mind. Because the mind is such a powerful source, from time to time, I like to give my mind a mental health day off work. This is done through the process of removing thoughts, ideas, concepts, fears, worries, doubt, and anything else going on in your headspace and writing it out on paper.

Writing is a way to escape, a sounding board, or some great form of release. The concept behind writing out your thoughts provides the opportunity to step outside of yourself and see with a fresh set of eyes. Writing things out helps you process and experience a set of choices made and visually discover whether or not those choices were purposeful or beneficial.

An amazing life coach and friend of mine refers to this process as *brain dumping*. The processing and maneuvering through the information you write out is where the true and real work begins. This allows you to categorize your thoughts, evaluate the relevance of those thoughts, prioritize the importance of the thoughts, and scrap the thoughts which are not beneficial, relevant, or productive toward your ultimate goal. The assumed ultimate goal is to live a fulfilling, purpose-driven, and balanced life. Once this process is complete you are well on your way to a clutter-free mind and a clutter-free life.

The next major step in this process is dedication and commitment to the process you have started. Consistency is key to maintaining this worry and stress-free life. Just as in many other areas of life such as dieting, habit making or breaking, potty training, or whatever you can fathom dedicating your time, physical and mental faculties to the way of life you desire is paramount. Make the choice to take back control of your clock today.

When considering things which are a priority, look at the thing you are considering the priority, and ask yourself a few questions. How will this affect my family or me? How will this be of benefit to either someone or myself? Is this moving me toward my long-term endeavor? Evaluating these questions with a transparent lens is the absolute best and most effective way of developing a conscious plan of action.

Be completely honest with yourself. Do you find yourself falling into the trap of busy work just to keep busy or is there real, tangible, and purposeful work behind what you are doing? Time is one thing in life we cannot get back. No one has the right or the power to dictate your time. You possess the power to use your time the way you desire.

THE **PROCRASTINATION** CYCLE

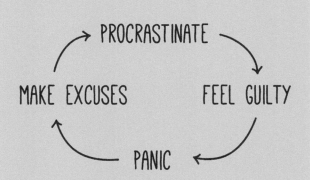

CHAPTER:

PROCRASTINATION AND
STAGNATION

03

As mentioned in the last chapter, time is a valuable and priceless gift. Don't waste it! Procrastination is defined by simply putting off something for a later time. The simple solution to changing this behavior is to simply *stop it*. Sounds easy enough, right? Wrong, procrastination, just as any other behavioral habit at times, become just that a habit.

For individuals caught in the habit of procrastinating, it is a way of life for them. This act is used as a way to escape psychologically from addressing issues considered stressful or daunting. Some people are even empowered by or motivated by the act of beating the clock. They're driven by their ability to work under pressure and get a thrill out of waiting until the very last minute. The danger in procrastination and stagnation is there is no margin for error.

One misquoted monetary amount on the bottom line of a small business can set you financially behind. The last minute submission of a dissertation allows no wiggle room for correction. Waiting until the last minute to pull the string on a parachute can have a devastating end. There are so many other scenarios in which play out just as fatal simply because we fail to plan and plan to fail.

To correct this problem, we need to develop a new behavioral pattern or habit. One that is realistic and attainable, exhibiting almost immediate results. Generally speaking, this is what we, as humans, desire a quick turnaround on our investment.

For starters, break up the task. Simplify what needs to get done and give yourself a little grace, understanding there are only twenty-four hours in a day, and you need to sleep at least six of those hours. When a task seems overwhelming or too massive to get done, the natural tendency is to delay. We doubt ourselves, we fear the process or the commitment, and we self-destruct.

More often than not, procrastination is the result of not knowing where to begin in the process of organizing your mind and life. If or perhaps when this occurs, don't allow the stress or trepidation to hold you back. Start at the beginning, re-center and refocus yourself, and move forward. Create a healthy habit or ritual consisting of things that motivate you. If there's a specific song, fragrance, or activity which invigorates you, engage those things. Aligning yourself with things you enjoy helps build the systematic approach needed for you to start and complete goals. To make it plain—we do what we enjoy.

The establishment and follow-through of something we oppose or are not interested in generally crashes and burns quickly. In moments of despair or feelings of doubt, give yourself a pep talk. Support systems are strongly encouraged, but sometimes in varying moments, all you have is you.

Self-motivation becomes a source within oneself, and it is up to you to inspire, encourage, and uplift yourself. Develop a mantra, a saying you can repeat to yourself during the process of task completion. Seriously! Remember the book *The Little Engine That Could* by Watty Piper? The Little Engine found itself burdened with the task of pulling a large freight up a steep hill. As this little train chugged and chugged up the hill, it repeated to itself, "I think I can, I think I can, I think I can." Why do you suppose this was the phrase selected for Thomas the Train? I can only imagine the writer of *The Little Engine That Could* had an understanding of how our mind works.

This understanding led to the recognition of the power we each individually possess in one thought. Use your words as your weapon to a healthy balance and goal completion. Another area where we self-destruct is asking for help. If you are anything like me asking for help is almost harder than pulling out your loose tooth. Yikes, right! However, if I were truly honest, I would tell you this was one of my greatest downfalls. Failing to ask for or receive help when offered stagnates, and at times dispels our dreams and goals.

I will let you in on a little secret no one told me until well, into my late thirties, ask for help when in need. I wish someone would have told me this years ago. Asking for help is one of the grand secrets to success in organizing your mind and your life. We were never meant to do life or things alone, and a helping hand is always appreciated. When considering asking for or accepting help, be realistic with yourself regarding your time, ability, competency, and any other important factors that exist.

A realistic outlook at the aforementioned areas will assist in minimizing or alleviating stress or feeling burdened by a specific task undertaken. Throughout the whole process of organizing, your mind and working through organizing your life, be completely transparent and honest with yourself whether you are facing a personal or professional decision to be made considered what is at stake.

Evaluate the task or opportunity holistically and ask yourself some of the same questions asked previously. How would this decision affect you? How will it affect your family? How will this affect your work? How will any of these areas or any other be affected by failing to complete a task or take on a specific project? More often than not, life will still go on, and the people around you will continue to maintain. Sometimes, all we need to do is sit our pride aside. We need to be willing to accept help and delegate where needed.

The final step in shifting from procrastination and stagnation to productive and purposeful is to treat yourself. Yes, pat yourself on the back and bid yourself a complimentary well-done or congratulations. This self-proclaimed pat on the back does not need to wait until you have reached the point of self-actualization. Small wins are still victories and should be celebrated. When you reach a milestone or accomplish a win, regardless of how small you view the win, celebrate you however you see fit.

04

CHAPTER:
TIME MANAGEMENT

04

The premise of this book is for you to take back your time and not allow the clock and its timing to run you. This is possible and attainable. However, this process is dictated by you. Some would argue, my career dictates my time, my spouse, my children, and on and on. I get it, many sources are pulling on us, and they all need a piece of our time. Some of those people or things need more time than others. In those cases, flexibility is warranted.

However, I can speculate if you were to think hard enough, there are areas where your time management poses a larger threat than the needs of other individuals or even work issues. The stress of managing your clock, not to mention the clock of your family and workplace, can make you want to take a sledgehammer to the clock once and for all. Morning routines, carpools, soccer, basketball practices, dance rehearsals, professional development meetings, and the list can go on and on.

Managing your time is simply an awareness of the fact, the clock exists. The goal is not to allow the clock to dictate your every move. Time management is almost a forethought of what you are going to do or need to do to prepare you for what's to come. The key to simplifying this is to tell your clock what you are going to do, what you will delegate, and what you will scratch off the list until another time. So much of what you have read throughout overlap the use of time management.

Establishing a timer system is an effective way to keep track of time usage. The use of a timer assists in heightening the conscious awareness of time. Generally, we allocate time to certain projects, activities, and events. Have you ever said, "I'm going to this event, but I'm only staying one hour?" This is an example of the timer system at work. Setting a timer and focusing on what is at stake at the moment can draw your focus and attention in and drive you toward beating the clock. The user of the timer system had the opportunity to see the time they have and appropriately use the time wisely.

Time management also means making your best yes decision. Best yes decisions, as referred to in an earlier chapter, are those decisions that work best to provide you with adequate mental, physical, and emotional security. Using the best yes approach at times will lead to you saying no. Honestly, I find it hard to say no at times. The request keeps coming, and I feel almost compelled to respond with a yes.

Imagine you are headed to a meeting and your notification signals, you have a text message from your sister. She was headed to work, and her tire blew, and she needs a ride to work. You have mentally sketched out your morning, and already, you are racing the clock. What are you drawn to do?

If this is not a scenario you're familiar with, I'm certain you have one that conveys the same message. The message is clear: our time is not our time until we start addressing the fundamental elements attempting to take over or control our time. If it is not your sibling, your spouse, or your neighbor it will be someone or something else. Everyone's crisis cannot always be your crisis.

05

CHAPTER:
HOW YOU START AND END

05

In the book, *The 7 Habits of Highly Effective People,* author Stephen Covey described seven habits according to this writing which is instrumental in creating habits to promote effective and productive living. Habit two, as expressed in the book is, "begin with the end in mind." Meaning, how you start anything is a clear depiction as to how you will end. When revamping your system or process to organize your life and find peace and rest, it is vital to approach things holistically.

Recognize where you are and decide where you are going before the process begins. Of course, it is not always fun to remove the spontaneity in life and settle for a plan. However, with a plan in place, you will be able to see the path you are on clearly and the direction you wish to go. This clarity in your path provides an opportunity for spontaneity and freedom from both the physical and mental pressures that exist within planning.

Plans are purposeful and useful. They are not always fail-safe, but I can assure you the lack of planning will result in failure. I would like us to consider a contractor who builds homes. This contractor does not decide to build a house without a blueprint and plan of what is needed to successfully build a house. A traveler does not simply get on a plane, get in a vehicle, or board a boat without some form of a concerted manifesto.

If you are truly seeking to obtain long-term or even transformative change through organization, it would behoove you to think through from start to possibly finish any possible outcomes and experiences you may encounter while journeying toward your purposeful and fulfilling life.

06

CHAPTER:
ESTABLISHING ROUTINES

06

Here, I would like to insert a quick disclaimer: with a household of seven people, routines are a must! Over the past several years, I have learned how valuable and priceless the establishment of routines are. We all have daily, weekly, and even monthly routines established.

Routine is defined as a set regimen or actions that are regularly followed. Whether it's getting up for work every morning at the same time, stopping by the same coffee shop to get your favorite hot caramel macchiato, making sure your kids go down for their afternoon nap, or dinner is on the table by 6:00 p.m. each night. Routines are something we engage in daily. More specifically, our daily routine serves the purpose of keeping us on track with our day-to-day processes. Routines warrant little to no variation.

The purpose of organization, as expressed throughout this book, is to expose the secrets which are not explicitly secret, just under spoken or unrecognized truths leading to a stress-free and balanced life. The goal is freedom from a cluttered schedule, which leads to a decluttered mind, emotion, and life. Adhering to routines foster the development of good habits. The establishment of good habits promotes movement and encourages us to move toward our ultimate goal or aspiration.

Efficient and effective routines provide greater opportunities to free up time and provide opportunities to spend more of your time doing what truly brings you peace and joy. I have intentionally used my two oldest children to establish a greater understanding of how to teach ability in the area of organization and routine work with children. They are both females ages nine and ten.

Since the birth of my children, I have implemented some form of routine. As infants, they had schedules for when they woke up in the morning, bathed, and so on. When they were able to recognize pictures, I made poster boards with pictures describing what they could expect for each day. As they aged, I continue the process of creating poster boards to give them a visual of what to expect and what was expected from them.

Now that they are older, without hesitation or even direction from me, they create and post the breakdown of their routine and their day. They are both avid list makers and have used calendars and planners at their request for the last few years now. I often joke with my husband saying, "We produce independent kids," of course, they still need reminders or motivation, but one thing I have learned and

I've taught my children is the act of providing grace and extending patience with yourself.

A common phrase used and heard is, "we are our worst critics," this phrase is extremely true. One major pitfall easily missed and easily experienced is falling into the snare of placing an extreme amount of pressure on yourself in any area of life. This is why we need to give ourselves grace and forgiveness at times. Do not take the grace you have provided yourself as an opportunity to not reach your established goal or aspiration. On the contrary, focus your attention on the goal at hand and use the grace given to be fully engaged in the journey life has you on.

An established routine helps you sleep easy at night and awaken refreshed and motivated to kick-start the day. The pressure of what do I have to do and where do I start my day is dismantled. To some degree, you can function on autopilot where what needs to get done gets done without the need to spin your wheels focused on what you should be doing. Routines are a source of calm in an undesired world of calamity.

07

CHAPTER:

THE SECRET UNLOCKED

07

Reaching for the stars has been an innate phenomenon for many of us since the onset of our viewing, these miraculous, celestial, incandescent, luminous points. There's absolutely nothing wrong with desiring to touch them, view them in a closer sense, or even admire the wonder of its creation. However, one could argue, are the stars even reachable?

The answer to this question is no. The stars that shimmer and shine so beautiful and angelic are so profoundly hot they would instantaneously destroy the human body if touched. Thus, why are we as human beings inundated with life's pressure of reaching for something we were never going to be able to truly ascertain? The world in which we live, just like the clock which seeks control over us, wants us to constantly strive and push until all we do in life is focused on what the world wants and what the clock dictates.

Sure, we exist within the world and hold dreams, aspirations, and desires. It is also true to some degree our clock is run by some outside entity such as school, work, families, and other factors. Although these truths are relevant, when did they become the sole purpose in life which affects our minds, bodies, and soul? When did we give the power and authority of our existence completely over to the outside world? One secret is we gave the clock its power when we stopped focusing on what we wanted and began believing what everyone else wanted for us or from us.

Here is the main secret you have anticipated from the beginning of this book. The purpose of life isn't to get it all done but to enjoy life along the way. We are constantly seeking balance and an understanding of how to get it all done and done well. But, the truth is we were never purposed or intended to get it all done and have balance. It is now up to us to choose our path of organization and a peaceful journey or submit ourselves to the overwhelming chaos that plagues us when we fail in one way or another.

Remember, the goal is to find balance not perfection. Perfection in anything is a hoax; it's a fallacy that seeks to destroy every ounce of mental, emotional, and physical stability we possess. Remember the best yes practice and prepare yourself to say yes to growth and no to a life of dictatorship by the clock. In doing this, you are yes to those things which nudge you forward and no to the things that leave you stagnant or feeling unfulfilled. If no one has told you lately let me be the first to say: YOU'VE GOT THIS! Let's make the conscious decision to take back control of our clock today!

About the Author

Ni'Tasha Liggins is a professional counselor and productivity consultant with an expertise in mental health, relationship, and organizational counseling, and consulting. She has over twelve years' experience in community mental health, as well as eleven years' experience as a domestic engineer. Her experience within these domains informs her relational and passionate approach.

Ni'Tasha is a wife and a mother of five children. This aspect of her life fuels her knowledge and determination to be creative, productive, and organized in all aspects of life. Her desire to get and stay organized ensures she is mentally, physically, and emotionally present in the most important areas of her life which are her family and community. Ni'Tasha lives by the mantra *Simple is always best*. Simplicity to her takes on a new purpose by inviting a new perspective and outlook to emerge by memories made and removing the bondage of busy work.

CPSIA information can be obtained
at www.ICGtesting.com
Printed in the USA
BVHW092012180421
605036BV00014B/1562

9 781662 430626